A SPIRIT DAUGHTER WORKBOOK

WRITTEN BY
JILL WINTERSTEEN

FOR THE FULL MOON

THURSDAY, JUNE 24TH, 2021
11:41 AM PDT

02

THE FULL MOON

Full Moons are powerful portals of self-discovery that occur each month. While New Moons begin the lunar cycle, Full Moons are the halfway point, when we have had two weeks to build, create and mold our dreams. It is during this phase that we begin to manifest our visions and embody a new version of ourselves. Full Moons are also a time to fully integrate new vibrations we've been creating and allow them to be seen and heard by others.

Community

Full Moons are very much about community. The light of the Moon throughout the night allows us to gather with others and bask in her reflected rays. If we follow the path of the Moon, the New Moon is the time to create the next version of ourselves; the Full Moon is the time to show that version to the world. It's a time to stand in our newly formed power to be seen differently and feel accepted for our changes. Setting intentions for ourselves is wonderful, but we need to embody and live those intentions around others. It can be daunting to show your new self to the world. But know it's ok to change and evolve. Allow others to see the real you and the energy you now hold. Watch their perceptions shift and their expectations of you to change. As your community begins to see the real you, it will feel like a weight has been lifted. You will be able to express yourself more authentically and embrace the person you are becoming.

Opposition

A Full Moon works with the power of opposition. During this phase, the Moon directly opposes the Sun. This aspect illuminates where our logical minds may not be aligning with our emotions and intuition. We can start to understand the barriers we have against truly listening to ourselves. We can discover where our doubts prevent us from expanding into who we wish to be. The Moon rules intuition, the ability to receive, and emotions. The Sun, on the other hand, represents the practical mind, the core personality, and the ability to react. When they oppose, we can feel where these parts of us create tension in our energy. The Full Moon is a time to recognize which side of you is running the show. Are you balanced? Or do you rely on logic so much that it dampens your ability to dream and receive gifts from the Universe? Or perhaps you could use more structure and logic to manifest your dreams. Each Full Moon provides an opportunity to check in and see if you need to balance the opposing Sun and Moon energies within your own field and help them work together, not against each one another.

Astrological Opposition

The Full Moon always sits in the opposing zodiac sign to the Sun. These astrological energies flavor our Full Moon and give us direction on what to work on within our consciousness. During a Full Moon, we can see all sides of the astrological signs involved, including their low sides, their high sides, and their polarity points. Low sides represent the shadows of the signs. They are the lower vibrations of the astrological signs and often show up in our field as a result of trauma, lack of awareness, and overall imbalance. High sides are the energies that represent the vibrations that align with the full potential of the zodiac signs. We can align with the high sides by bringing them to the forefront of our awareness, where we can develop them and understand what they feel like. The Full Moon shows us the low side and the high side of each astrological energy involved within us. It then teaches us how to find balance, or the polarity point, where the low sides are shed and the high sides are integrated. In this integration, the energy has the potential to take on an even higher vibration than either sign could achieve alone.

The Full Moon is a powerful time for bringing awareness to what you need to release in order to achieve true balance in your energy. During each Full Moon, always ask yourself what energy you are trying to fully understand, balance, and integrate. Then get ready to release what no longer serves you and embrace your highest potential. The New Moon is the time to plant intentions; the Full Moon is when you have the opportunity to do the work needed to manifest those intentions. It can be an intense time emotionally, but ultimately it opens the door for a new way of being, feeling, and inspiring others.

CAPRICORN FULL MOON

Capricorn is the container for the ocean summoned by Cancer. As we begin to move through Cancer Season, this Full Moon gives us a perspective on our feelings and a place to put them. Capricorn is the steadfast goat of the zodiac. This energy gives us focus and motivation, and helps us develop self-discipline. Capricorn is the vibration we call in when creating routines, structures, and boundaries within ourselves.

Traditionally, Capricorn is associated with work, career, and reputation. While issues around your career may arise this Full Moon, attempt to expand your definition of work. Capricorn, at its core, represents your life's work. This may or may not have anything to do with your actual job. Your life's work may be a hobby, a child, your garden, or your daily meditation practice. As we move through this Full Moon, allow your consciousness to explore the different types of work in your life. Then align with this Full Moon to commit to paths that embody your soul's mission.

Capricorn wants each of us to live a life of purpose. Your purpose is something that comes from deep within your soul. It is how you extend the roots of your being into

CAPRICORN FULL MOON

the world. Capricorn is also associated with integrity. This energy wants us to show up in the world standing firmly in our truth. It challenges us to be the same person no matter where we are, who we are with, or what situation arises. Furthermore, having integrity means we interact with the world consistently in a way that matches our core ideals and beliefs. When we are fully aligned with Capricorn, we live a purposeful life that resonates with our core values. We extend our truth into the world from a firm foundation rooted in the soul.

The Capricorn Full Moon is a time to go within and understand your core essence. It's a time to commit to finding your purpose and shed anything that distracts you, including your emotions. Your feelings are important to pay attention to and understand, but Capricorn asks that you see them as information. They do not define you, but they can give you clues to what is most important to you. Emotions are a doorway to finding out who you are and what matters most to your soul.

Over this Full Moon, commit to practices and disciplines that help you understand your emotions and, in turn, understand yourself. These practices then become boundaries with yourself. They are times you set aside each day to explore your feelings. In doing so, you'll give yourself space to feel but will also give your emotions a container. When you know you have space to explore your emotions, they are less likely to show up and distract your focus.

It's also important to acknowledge that your self-care practices are productive. Capricorn helps us define our meaning of productivity. It's not just to-do lists and checkboxes. Taking care of ourselves and our emotions helps us move forward in life with ease. This ease extends to work and to-do lists. On this Capricorn Moon, make taking care of yourself a priority, and know that everything else in your life will benefit when you are replenished. This Moon is very much about creating a true work/life balance and understanding the interconnection of everything you do. While it may not feel like you are getting anything done on a day spent "doing nothing," you are actually restoring your spirit and recharging your mind. You then have the power to meet your future tasks from a restored place versus a depleted one.

Release any unnecessary pressure you put on yourself this Full Moon. Shift your expectations of what you need to get done to feel worthy of a break. We often don't think we deserve time off from our work until we can get x, y, and z done. In truth, you deserve time to rest and restore whenever you need it. Learn to listen to yourself and your needs this Full Moon. Let go of any guilt that occurs when you take a day off. Giving yourself space away from your work helps you appreciate it and shift it if needed. You have time to discover your true life's work and adjust your work accordingly. If you are already immersed in your soul's calling, a break will restore your love for it. It will renew your passion and inspire you to keep going. If you haven't found your life's work yet, a break from your daily tasks will give you time to hear your intuition and let it lead you to your purpose. Taking time for yourself is one of the most productive things you can do. So remember that during this Full Moon as you feel into your soul's mission.

This Full Moon is also a wonderful time to revisit the intentions you set on the New Moon in Capricorn. What practices and disciplines have helped you these past six months? What commitments need to shift? Are you committing your energy to something that no longer needs it? While commitments are important, releasing some to make room for new ones aligned with who you are now is also important. Take the opportunity provided by this Full Moon to release anything in your life that distracts you from your true purpose. Then make new commitments that align with who you are, what's most important to you, and the person you want to be.

CAPRICORN MOON X CANCER SUN

While the Moon sits in Capricorn, the Sun sits in Cancer, bringing us an opportunity to balance both of these vibrations in our energetic body. Every energy has a low side and a high side. The extreme, or shadow, sides of Cancer and Capricorn are where they differ. Their higher sides contain commonalties. Through releasing the parts of ourselves aligned with the lower frequencies of these signs, we can align and integrate their higher ones. This integration gives us a new frequency to embody, which is higher than either sign individually. If we imagine a line of energy, the lower vibrations of Cancer sit at one end, and the lower vibrations of Capricorn sit at the other. As we walk away from these extreme sides, toward the center, we find a balance point where their higher vibrations merge to form a greater whole.

On this Full Moon, go inward and identify where you are attached to the shadow side of each sign and release those attachments. In doing so, you will bring balance to your energy and open the path to a higher vibration. Capricorn and Cancer form an axis of energy concerned with responsibility and authenticity. Where Cancer wants us to be responsible to ourselves, Capricorn wants us to be responsible to others. Both signs, though, want us to show up in our truth always.

Cancer sits in the fourth house of the home. It represents the part of our consciousness that only we see. This part includes our imagination, our intuition, and our fantasies. It also includes our deep-seated emotions, such as fear, insecurity, anxiety, and all of our shadows. The fourth house is the lowest point on the zodiac wheel, which represents true darkness and our deepest subconscious thoughts. In this space, we have only ourselves to rely upon, with our intuition as our only guiding light.

Cancer is ruled by Water and the Moon. This energy is connected to everything and feels intensely. The higher vibration of Cancer reminds us that we are all one, with no boundaries separating us. When we align with this side, we understand that when we give energy, we also receive it and vice versa. We uphold our responsibility to take care of ourselves because we know when we do so, we take care of those around us. Through self-care, we easily connect with our intuition and the knowledge of the Universe. From a place of restoration, we effortlessly feel universal wisdom, understanding that we are everything and everything is us. We feel connected to our core and make decisions from our inner guidance with confidence and ease. Life flows, and we flow with it, always knowing that our inner compass is finely tuned.

The lower vibration of Cancer forgoes the responsibility to oneself and, in turn, forgets the connection to everything in the Universe. When we attach to this vibration of Cancer, we forget to take care of ourselves and lose our ability to care for others. We end up feeling detached from the world around us, unsupported, and alone. We may even be numb or emotionally arrested. We can also fall into the trap of emotional neediness, ego, and insecurity from the desire to feel connected to others and ourselves. As we separate from our emotions, we lose touch with our intuition,

CAPRICORN MOON X CANCER SUN

not knowing which path to take next. We begin to feel overwhelmed by life and its many decisions. Without our inner guidance, we fall into a trap overthinking and overanalyzing. We may feel there is no safe space for ourselves. The lower vibrations of Cancer can lead to emotional and life burnout. They can make you feel overwhelmed, tired, needy of others, and emotionally out of control. If you feel these lower vibrations show up in your life, it's best to take self-care time. Carve out space each day to sit with yourself, take a vacation, or take a day to connect with nature. Be honest about your needs and be open to receiving what you need. Give yourself the love you deserve, and remember that your first responsibility is to yourself.

Capricorn, on the other hand, looks at our responsibilities to the world outside ourselves. Home in the tenth house, which sits at the top of the zodiac wheel, Capricorn shows us the pieces of our energy we project outwardly and allow us to see the light. Capricorn is ruled by Earth and Saturn, which ground our energy and inspire us to make healthy choices rooted in wisdom. Capricorn is concerned with what we contribute to society and how we show up in the world. Capricorn also sees the world as a connected whole. This energy understands that when we build systems and make rules for others from a feeling of oneness, we take care of everyone. Capricorn gives a model for a truly integrated society, where the leaders see themselves in everyone and make decisions for the good of all.

When we align with Capricorn's higher vibrations, we show up authentically in the world, revealing our true selves to those around us. We do not judge others, nor do we fear being judged. We understand the connection with everyone around us. We also make it a priority to do the work needed to stay in an authentic place. We know who we are, and we show up as this person in every situation. We commit to staying aligned with intuition and clearing out any blocks that distract us from our life's mission. Once connected to our internal wisdom, we make decisions for ourselves and others from this place. We courageously live from our cores and steering our lives with our hearts.

The lower vibrations of Capricorn, like Cancer, also make us feel detached and alone. In this feeling of isolation, we forgo our responsibility to the world around us and become preoccupied with power, success, and reputation. We place too much emphasis on what others think about us and end up in a vibration of judgment because we feel judged. We become driven by the ego and forget that we are one with everyone around us. We lose sight of what is most important and place superficial things above what makes our hearts truly happy. If we happen to be a leader and fall into a lower vibration of Capricorn, we make decisions that serve ourselves and our control of power instead of creating systems that serve the good of all people.

The lower vibrations of Capricorn can also lead to burnout, where we overwork ourselves and forget to take care of our needs. It's the making of late nights and forgotten dinners for the sake of completing a project. We exhaust ourselves and forget the priority of self-care. If you find yourself aligning with the lower side of Capricorn, take some time for yourself. Give yourself a day off and forget about your to-do lists. Also, do something for someone else. Give your time and energy selflessly to being present with another person. Give and receive as you feel the interconnectedness of life itself.

When we create harmony between Cancer and Capricorn, we find our foundation rooted in what matters most to us. We also hear our intuition. Our inner compass becomes free of disrupting emotions and shows us how to spend our time. We create balance in our lives, making time for self-care, work, friends, and passion. We tend carefully to our needs and the needs of others. We understand the connection of all beings and make decisions for the unified collective. The integration of these energies allows us to nourish our roots while making sure our branches match them.

ASPECTS

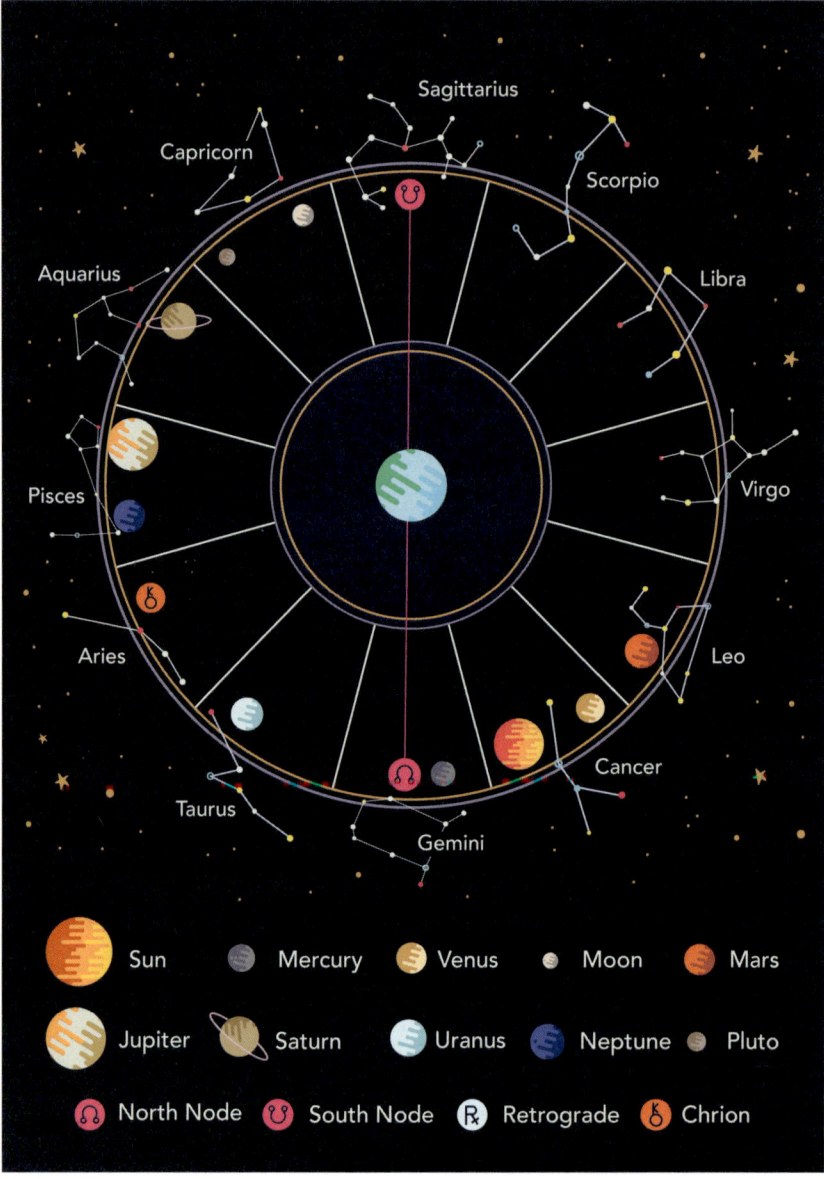

The main aspect of every Full Moon is the opposite of the Sun and Moon. Oppositions reveal energies. In this revelation, they stir up tension and lead to an energetic breakthrough. They can make us feel impatient, on the verge of a breakdown, and restless in our bodies. The key to working with any opposition is to allow it. Allow the information to come through and open yourself to new realties. What we resist always persists, and it usually grows exponentially in its presence. Fighting against the energies of the Full Moon leads to sleepless nights, irritation, and even fatigue. When working with the Full Moon, it's best to face the energies with courage and an open heart. Then allow them to take you on a journey of self-discovery and healing.

ASPECTS

In addition the Full Moon opposite, we have one other major aspect this day with Jupiter in Pisces: the Moon forms a sextile aspect with Jupiter, and the Sun forms a trine aspect. Sextiles and trines are beneficial aspects. They bring harmony to the energies involved. Jupiter's vibrations are added to the vibrations of the Full Moon, elevating them.

Jupiter is currently stationed retrograde in Pisces. Jupiter is quite happy in Pisces, as this planet is the traditional ruler of the fish. Jupiter expands energy and reminds us of our potential. It is also the planet of luck and abundance. In Pisces, Jupiter helps us dream even bigger. It reminds us that we are infinite beings with infinite potential. There is nothing we can't achieve, and no dream is too big. This transit helps us break down self-imposed limitations and manifest our greatest dreams. It asks us to stop playing small and take up space with our visions.

In retrograde, Jupiter allows us to see that happiness, luck, and abundance are an inside job. We can attract anything we want in this world and manifest any dream. BUT, we have to believe. We have to embody the energy we wish to attract. We have to be it before we receive it. Jupiter retrograde in Pisces encourages us to live as if our dreams have already become a reality. It encourages us to address places of self-doubt and their origins. Is it possible for you to believe your dreams have already occurred? Is there a part of you that doesn't believe you are capable of manifesting your visions? Is there a part of you that sells yourself short and squanders your potential?

This Full Moon is the time to confront underlying beliefs around what you think is possible in your life. If you don't believe it can occur, then it won't. On the contrary, if you live like what you desire is already here, then what you desire will manifest with brilliance. As Jupiter adds its energy to this Full Moon, feel what work you need to do to live your most extraordinary life. What great life's work are you ready to accomplish and how can you make it your daily reality? What do you need to release? What do you need to nourish? What do you need to believe is possible?

Houses

The following section is composed of horoscopes based on your house. Just as cosmic bodies interact with each other, they also interact with your natal chart. The Full Moon moves through, or transits, an area of your chart. Your astrological chart is a picture of the sky when you were born. There are planets, signs, and houses. The twelve houses divide the sky and your chart into twelve pieces. Each piece represents a part of your life. Your houses are governed by an astrological sign. The planets then land in the different houses.

We each have a house that is contacted, in some part, by Capricorn. This is the part of your chart the Full Moon in Capricorn is transiting, or moving through. When the Full Moon transits an area of your chart, it activates it, whether there is a planet present or not. You do not need to have any cosmic bodies in Capricorn to feel the effects of this Full Moon. We will all feel them, and we will feel them in the area of our chart governed by Capricorn. Understanding your houses is the key to understanding how each Full Moon will affect you.

HouseScopes give guidance on what to focus on this Full Moon determined by which house is governed by Capricorn. You can look up your chart at astro-charts.com. Look to the outer edge of your chart to find Capricorn. Then look to the inner wheel to find the house number. If you'd like to be even more precise, find 3° Capricorn (the start of Capricorn closest to Sagittarius). This degree is the exact location of the Full Moon. Find the house this degree falls in and focus your Full Moon work on this area of your life.

HOUSESCOPES

First House Capricorn: Your first house helps form your identity. It informs your choices and guides your life decisions. It's also how you project yourself to the world. With Capricorn governing this house, you appear responsible, focused, and committed. You may not feel this way, but that's how others see you. With the Full Moon transiting this house, focus your attention on how you want to be seen. How do you want to define your identity? And what do you need to shift so that others see you as you really are?

Second House Capricorn: Your second house governs how you interact with possessions, finances, and your self-worth. It represents your emotional, physical, and energetic resources. With Capricorn governing this house, you have a desire to discipline yourself in regards to finances. You want to be responsible with your resources. Even if you haven't accomplished it yet, it is a priority in your life. With the Full Moon transiting this house, release any unworthiness. Realize that the only practice you need to create abundance is believing you are worthy of it. Challenge yourself to feel abundant and allow yourself to call it in.

Third House Capricorn: Your third house governs how you communicate and the choices you make when speaking, listening, and opening your mind. It represents how you actively exchange information with the world. With Capricorn governing this house, you are clear and concise in your communication. You may even be seen as terse or short in the way you speak. With the Full Moon transiting this house, expect issues to arise around your communication and perceptions. How can you expand your vision and invite new perspectives to help you create a more balanced life?

Fourth House Capricorn: Your fourth house governs your home, including your subjective world. It rules the area of your life only you know—the part you may find challenging to explain to others. With Capricorn leading this house, you tend to keep your struggles to yourself. You may find it hard to ask for help or to accurately share your needs. With the Full Moon transiting this house, take the opportunity to dissolve some of your walls and let others into your world. Ask for what you need and allow yourself to receive it.

Fifth House Capricorn: Your fifth house governs your creative expression and what you do for recreation. It also influences how you interact with your inner child. With Capricorn ruling this house, you may at times forget the importance of play. Be aware when you become too serious about life, and remember to laugh at yourself from time to time. With the Full Moon transiting this house, dissolve any rigidity in your schedule and make time to enjoy life. See the world for the playground it is and have fun.

Sixth House Capricorn: Your sixth house governs how you give your gifts to the world. It guides you in serving others and feeling good enough to share your talents. With Capricorn in this house, you make service part of your life's mission and work. Your career may even revolve around giving your gift to elevate the planet. With the Full Moon transiting this house, expect issues to arise around your life's work. Is it fulfilling your need to be of service? Is there anything you need to adjust or bring into balance?

You can look up what house Capricorn rules in your chart, at astro-charts.com

HOUSESCOPES

Seventh House Capricorn: Your seventh house governs your relationships and how you show up in them. With Capricorn here, you are committed and loyal. Just be aware if you made the relationship with your work a priority over your relationships with people. With the Full Moon transiting this house, take the opportunity to look at your commitments. Who and what are you committed to? Dissolve any obligations that are outdated or that distract you from your life's purpose.

Eighth House Capricorn: Your eighth house governs your personal growth and expansion. It guides how you interact with the lessons life brings you. With Capricorn ruling this house, your career may shift and change throughout your life. With these changes, it brings you growth if you are willing to accept and see the lessons. As the Full Moon transits this house, transform past pain or trauma into power that can propel you forward. Focus on self-care and restore your spirit this Full Moon. This replenishment will help you integrate your rapid growth.

Ninth House Capricorn: Your ninth house governs your travels and how you integrate new knowledge. With Capricorn ruling this house, your life's work includes traveling to new places and exploring new lands. For your growth, it's important to expose yourself to different cultures and ideas. As the Full Moon transits this house, find balance in your work and life through new experiences. Give yourself self-care through new ideas and people who expand you. Let these new perspectives bring together all aspects of your life.

Tenth House Capricorn: Your tenth house governs your career and your life's work. It is the house traditionally ruled by Capricorn. With Capricorn ruling this house for you, your work takes center stage in your life. Just make sure what you do for a job lines up with your soul's work. What mission are you here to accomplish? As the Full Moon transits this house, take the opportunity to evaluate your career path. Let go of anything that doesn't feel aligned with your life's purpose and focus on what resonates with your heart.

Eleventh House Capricorn: Your eleventh house governs your friends and acquaintances. It guides how you interact with your community, and even lead it. With Capricorn ruling this house, you are a natural leader. You can organize any gathering—large or small. You don't make the best follower but are exceptional at mobilizing those around you. As the Full Moon transits this house, expect issues to arise with your relationship with the collective. Are you showing up in your power? Are you showing up with compassion? What needs to shift this Full Moon to balance your natural leadership skills?

Twelfth House Capricorn: Your twelfth house governs your spiritual path. With Capricorn ruling this house, you need solitude and space for your spiritual endeavors. You are committed to your practices and have a high level of self-discipline when it comes to yoga, meditation, and other rituals. As the Full Moon transits this house, feel into the magic of the day. What is it teaching you? Where can you take more breaks, and where can you commit even more of your attention? Take some time today to meditate with nature and connect to the grounded energy of the planet.

You can look up what house Capricorn rules in your chart, at astro-charts.com

CAPRICORN LUNAR FLOW

Capricorn provides us with very grounding energy, creating stillness and focus. On her Full Moon, harness this energy within by practicing yoga postures that connect you with this Earth energy. Through the practice of breath observation and bodily stillness, we can align with the focused energy of Capricorn. This sequence is designed to help you feel grounded and strong throughout your body and mind.

Mountain Pose
Begin by standing at the top of the mat, with feet together and eyes closed. Slightly rotate your palms forward as you stand tall through your spine and crown of your head. Root your feet into the ground as you breathe deeply. Inhale for a count of 4, then exhale for a count of 4. Repeat this breath for about a minute as you feel into your body and the present moment.

Half Moon Standing Variation
Open your eyes, and on your inhale, reach your arms overhead. Clasp your left wrist with your right hand. On exhale, side bend to the right, keeping a firm footing on the ground. Breathe with the same 4-count for 5 breaths, lengthening through your left side. On inhale, lift your torso and slowly switch sides.

Forward Bend
Inhale and reach your arms overhead; on exhale, slowly fold forward, hinging at your hips. Press your feet into the ground and firm up your legs as you let your torso and neck relax. Feel the strength of your lower body as you release your upper body. Breathe here for 5 breaths.

Downward Dog
From the Forward Bend, walk your feet back into Downward Dog. Press your inner thighs back as you root into your heels. Feel your hands and feet on the Earth, balancing your body as you stretch your spine. After 5 breaths, walk your legs back up into a Forward Bend. Inhale and lengthen through your back; exhale and fold forward. Inhale and come back to standing with your hands on your hips.

Warrior 1 > Warrior 2 > Wide-Angle Forward Bend > Warrior 2 > Warrior 1
From the top of your mat, step your right foot back into Warrior 1. Have your back foot angled at 45 degrees as you bend into your front knee. Reach your arms up overhead as you breathe for 4 counts on inhale, then exhale. Hold for 5 breaths, then, on exhale, open up your hips to the right for Warrior 2. Reach your arms out to either side and adjust your back foot out a bit. Bend into your front knee, breathing deeply as you focus your attention on your front hand. Take 5 breaths here, stretching your hips. On inhale, straighten your front leg and parallel your feet for a

CAPRICORN LUNAR FLOW

Wide-Angle Forward Bend. With your hands on your hips, inhale and reach your spine upward, then exhale and fold over your legs. Release your hands to the ground and breathe for 5 long breaths, firming up through your legs. On inhale, place your hands on your hips and come back up to standing. Turn your right foot forward and repeat Warrior 1 and 2 on this side. Then come back to standing.

Triangle > Extended Side Angle > Wide Forward Bend

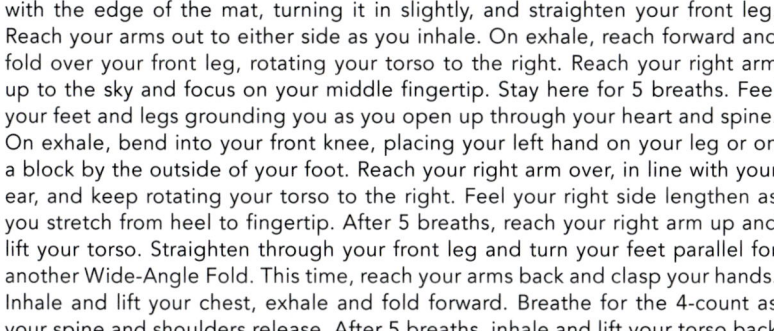

Step your right foot back for Triangle Pose. Have your back foot almost parallel with the edge of the mat, turning it in slightly, and straighten your front leg. Reach your arms out to either side as you inhale. On exhale, reach forward and fold over your front leg, rotating your torso to the right. Reach your right arm up to the sky and focus on your middle fingertip. Stay here for 5 breaths. Feel your feet and legs grounding you as you open up through your heart and spine. On exhale, bend into your front knee, placing your left hand on your leg or on a block by the outside of your foot. Reach your right arm over, in line with your ear, and keep rotating your torso to the right. Feel your right side lengthen as you stretch from heel to fingertip. After 5 breaths, reach your right arm up and lift your torso. Straighten through your front leg and turn your feet parallel for another Wide-Angle Fold. This time, reach your arms back and clasp your hands. Inhale and lift your chest, exhale and fold forward. Breathe for the 4-count as your spine and shoulders release. After 5 breaths, inhale and lift your torso back upright. Release your hands and rotate your feet to practice on the other side.

Mountain Pose

Step your feet back to the front of the mat to revisit Mountain Pose. Close your eyes and use the 4-count breath to re-center your awareness. Feel each inhale expand you and each exhale ground you, connecting you with the stability of the Earth.

Tree Pose

Float your eyes open and press down into your left foot. Slowing bring your right foot up for Tree Pose, placing it on the inside of your left leg. Press firmly down through your standing leg. Imagine roots going down into the Earth, providing you with stability and balance. Reach and lengthen your spine upward, growing taller through your torso as you lift your arms to the sky. Take 5 deep breaths here before switching sides.

Forward Bend

After Tree Pose, slowly come down to seated. Place a blanket or pillow under your hips and extend your legs out in front of you. Flex through your feet and straighten through your legs. Inhale and reach your arms up to the sky. As you exhale, fold over your legs as you lengthen through your back. With every inhale, reach through your spine, and with every exhale, fold a bit deeper. Stay here for 5 to 7 breaths, feeling the ground beneath you and allowing your mind to settle.

Twist

Come up slowly from the Forward Bend and lie down on your back. Gently hug both knees into your chest. Twist them over the right as you extend out through your arms. Expand your ribs on each inhale, and twist deeper on exhale. Spend 5 breaths here, then lift your knees back up and over to the other side.

Savasana - 5 mins

Extend both legs out on the ground. Feel your body completely supported, and allow this support to relax your body and mind. Return to a natural breath and observe the flow of inhale and exhale as you rest.

FULL MOON MEDITATION

The energy of Capricorn is all about focus and concentration. To fully align with her Full Moon, we want our mind settled and our thoughts organized. To help achieve this, practice the following breath meditation. Through placing attention on the breath, we sharpen the mind and allow it to clear. Practice this meditation during the Eclipse and on the days leading up to it.

Counting the Breath

Begin in a comfortable seated position. You can sit on a bolster or blanket to help lengthen your spine. Attempt to observe the breath through the exercise, allowing it to stay natural as you count. With your eyes closed, place your attention on your inhale and exhale. Count each breath until you get to 8. Inhale "1," exhale "2," inhale "3," exhale "4," and so on. Once you reach 8, return to 1. If you lose track of your count at any time, return to 1. Continue this for 5 minutes.

Say the Breath

Still seated with your eyes closed, let the numbers fade away. Say to yourself, "Inhale" on the inhale, and "Exhale" on the exhale. Continue to let the breath be natural, just observing it as it goes in and out of your body. Feel your mind beginning to focus and your concentration sharpening. Continue saying "Inhale" and "Exhale" with the breath for 5 minutes.

Observe the Breath

Remain seated with your eyes closed. Let the numbers fade away and focus all of your attention on the sensation of the breath. Follow the breath, feeling each sensation of the inhale and exhale. Concentrate your awareness on each nostril, feeling a subtle expansion and contraction with the breath. Focus on your rib cage, feeling its rise and fall, maybe even noticing a relaxation of muscles following the exhale. Allow your mind to become completely immersed in the feeling of the breath. Allow the breath to be the only sensation in your awareness. Continue this for 5 minutes.

Afterward, slowly open your eyes and feel the stillness you've created in your body, mind, and energy. Feel the clarity in your energy and the ability to focus on any task that comes your way.

FULL MOON SET UP

CIRCLE SET UP

On this Full Moon, we are working with the elements of Earth, from Capricorn, and Water, from Cancer. Water and Earth together create mud, which is deeply detoxifying and fertile. These elements, along with the energy of the Full Moon, provide a potent night to clear away old energies and create new ones. Feel into these elements when creating your space. Choose a space that feels grounded and connected to Mother Earth. You can practice outside close to the ground, or choose a space that contains the Wood element. If these are not available to you, place plants and crystals in your circle to bring the Earth inside. You can also practice alone, or in community. It's entirely up to you.

Incorporate the rest of the elements along with the Earth element. If possible, build a fire outside, which you can use later for releasing energy. You can also light candles in your space. For Air, incorporate auric sprays, have some feathers to fan the smudge sticks, or use a an oil diffuser. Place crystals in the middle of the circle and around the perimeter. Crystals that align with the energy of Capricorn are Malachite, Fluorite, and Garnet. They will help ground your energy and bring you clarity. Crystals for Cancer are Moonstone, Selenite, and Rose Quartz. They will help you love yourself unconditionally as you feel your emotions. You can also incorporate flowers of both Capricorn and Cancer into your space, including holly, lilies, hydrangeas and white roses. Bring in the element of Water through a vase or a metal bowl containing water. Gather all of your supplies and build your circle.

Create an outline with your objects, anchoring the four directions—North, South, East, and West—with either a crystal or candle. If you are creating an altar, set it up in the westerly part of the circle, as this direction helps energies release. Once the perimeter is set, cleanse the area with a dried herb. Cedar makes an excellent choice for this night, as it is grounding and clearing. Begin cleansing at the easterly point, moving to the South, West, North, then back to the East. Imagine a white light encasing the circle, protecting it from any external energies. Before your guests enter, cleanse each one of them and then yourself with a dried herb. Once you all have entered the circle, pause for a moment to let the energy settle before you begin.

Follow your intuitive guidance when leading a circle. Begin with each member introducing themself. Talk about the astrological energy of the day and how it is affecting each one of you. Share and learn from each other about your unique experiences with this Full Moon, giving plenty of space for each person to speak. Follow your conversation with the meditation practice in this book to calm the mind. You can then explore the rest of the practices. Do them alone and share as much, or as little, with the rest of the group as you'd like. Go over the questions and continue to learn from each other's perspectives.

After you've completed the practices in this workbook, set up for a releasing ritual. Grab an object that you don't mind letting go of. This can be a rock, a piece of broken crystal, or a flower. Hold the object in your hand and energetically send any vibration you no longer want in your field into the object's field. Feel the thought, emotion, or frequency transfer from you into the object. Then release the object into a body of water or bury it in the ground. Feel yourself cleansed of whatever you did not want as it completely leaves your energy. End the circle by giving thanks to everyone who attended and to yourself for showing up.

CARD READING

Reading Cards is a beautiful way to access your intuition and tap into your, and the Universe's, higher wisdom. Anyone can pull cards, as long as you are willing to receive the information they provide. You need no prior experience, or training, just an open and clear mind.

You may use any cards you like for this practice, including but not limited to: Tarot Cards, Animal Medicine Cards, Oracle Cards or any Affirmation Cards. You also can pull cards from a few decks to gain different perspectives. If you are new to card pulling, try to ask only one deck the same question, as asking different decks the same question can become quite confusing. Below are some general guidelines on how to pull cards. Please improvise as needed and above anything else, listen to your intuition.

Clear Your Mind
A settled, grounded mind is essential for pulling cards. The last thing you want is random thoughts running around when you are trying to receive clear answers from yourself. Practice the breath work and meditation in this workbook to prepare and settle your mind. You may also clear your mind using sound frequencies through singing bowls. These can either be crystal or metal bowls. Play the bowl, or bowls, for about 3-5 minutes to help rid your mind of external noise as you focus on the harmony of the sound.

CARD READING

Pick Your Deck
There are many different decks out there. You can choose as many as you like. Know, though, that they each provide you a different energy or medicine. Tarot Cards are the most popular and should be used carefully. Although very useful, Tarot cards can give the wrong impression if you interpret them harshly. Animal Medicine cards offer different types of messages from the animal realm which can help align with the spirit of nature. These cards give you the medicine you need to apply to your situation or question. Affirmation cards provide you with guidance in the form of words or phrases. When reading these cards, it is best to meditate on what the affirmation means for you. It is also helpful to repeat the affirmation a few times and see how it makes you feel. There are many other cards you can experiment with, like Goddess Cards, Angel Cards, and so on. The important thing to remember with any card is that they each have different angles and sides. There are often a few interpretations of the same card.

Shuffle
Shuffle the cards the easiest way for you. Some cards are smaller and can be shuffled like a regular deck of playing cards, while others with take some effort. If all else fails, spread them out on the floor in front of you then regather them. Keep a clear mind while shuffling. You can also repeat " I am open to receiving guidance and intuition." Refrain from asking your questions until the next step.

Capricorn Card Questions
You are free to ask the deck any questions you need answers to on this Full Moon. The following questions are meant to help you harness the energy of Capricorn through the cards to clarify some of these energies in your mind. This is a three-part card reading, where you'll ask the deck three questions. Before beginning, spread your freshly shuffled cards in a wide arc in front of you. Use your left middle finger to choose the card, first waving your hand slowly over the cards. You'll feel a magnetic pull, or slight tingle, in your fingertip when you hover over the right card. Chose one card at a time, taking a moment to breathe in between questions. Keep the cards flipped over until you pull all three.

What energy will help me release anything not aligned with my life's work?

What energy will help me align with my truth and core essence?

What energy will help me elevate my vision of productivity and give me true life balance?

Take Them In
Once you have your cards, flip them over. Before looking up their meaning, sit with them for a moment and allow them to speak to you. Intuit your own meaning and interpretation of the card. What is the card trying to tell you? What are you trying to tell yourself? After a few moments with the cards, look up their meaning. Sit with that information, merging it with your intuitive meaning of the cards.

As with everything, enjoy this process. Do not worry if you are doing it right or wrong. Just follow your intuition, and trust the journey. Accept the cards you are dealt and use their energy wisely to help guide you when you need it the most.

CAPRICORN PRACTICES

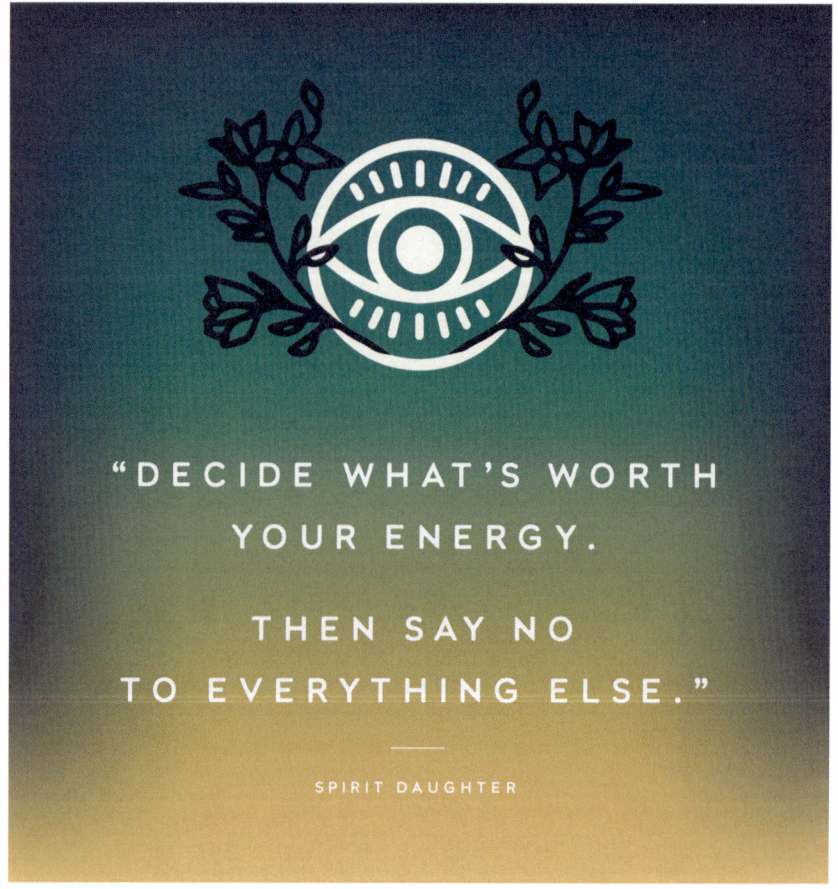

"DECIDE WHAT'S WORTH YOUR ENERGY.

THEN SAY NO TO EVERYTHING ELSE."

SPIRIT DAUGHTER

On this Full Moon, we are working with the energies of both Capricorn and Cancer. We have the opportunity to find a full integration of their highest frequencies and elevate our consciousness to the next level. Capricorn and Cancer teach us two sides of the same coin. Cancer reminds us to be responsible to ourselves, while Capricorn teaches us to be responsible to other people. These responsibilities are an interconnected loop that feed each other. When we give ourselves attention and make self-care a priority, we understand ourselves at the deepest level. We feel our core essence, including our priorities, values, and strengths. We also feel our soul's purpose. We can then take this knowledge and give it the world through our work. This work includes many more actions other than our job. It includes our passions, our contribution to raising the vibration of the planet, and the work we do to become more evolved.

When we understand ourselves at the deepest level, we can show that person to the world. We find authenticity in everything we do, and we show up in every situation as our true self. What we project outwardly matches what we feel inwardly. We also can clearly feel our intuition and find ways to follow it in every situation. We steer our lives from an inner compass, and we make commitments to others from this place. When we do the work needed to become clear in ourselves, we strengthen our impact on the world. We make firm decisions rooted in deep knowledge of our truths and what we are capable of achieving.

CAPRICORN PRACTICES

Throughout this Full Moon, feel into your inner truths. Commit to understanding yourself—past your emotions and deep into your core. Focus on finding the path to your intuition. Give yourself time and self-care, upholding your responsibility to yourself and learn what you can truly give to others. Also learn what you are willing to commit your energy to. What can you give yourself through the most challenging times while still finding love for what you are doing daily?

At the highest vibration of Capricorn and Cancer, there is no separation between you and others. What is good for you is good for everyone. Taking care of yourself takes care of the world. Healing yourself heals the world, raises your vibration, and raises the world's vibration. Feel into this connection and allow it to help release the lower vibrations of Capricorn and Cancer. The lower vibrations of Capricorn cause us to view success as a status symbol, where we tick off arbitrary boxes until we appear to have it all. We prioritize money, power, and control of resources, working ourselves to exhaustion until we have these things. We remain overly concerned with how others perceive us and allow only certain pieces of our personalities to shine through. Much of our true selves remain hidden in the shadow side, and we may even take on personas that do not match our core values. In many ways, the lower side of Capricorn is what conventional society views as successful. It is devoid of real connection, fulfillment, and higher purpose. When we step into this shadow side, we become judgmental of ourselves and those around us, isolating ourselves from the infinite energy of the Universe. We lose touch with what really matters, and we ignore our intuition.

The shadow side of Cancer shows up as neediness, codependency, and people-pleasing. When we take on this vibration of Cancer, we need others to need us. We place too much importance on taking care of those around us and forget to take care of ourselves. We put ourselves at the bottom of our to-do list and often ignore our own emotions for the sake of tending to another's. We may even suppress our emotions, causing a variety of illnesses in ourselves. We also lose touch with our intuition, forgetting the power it holds. Without it, we cannot make clear decisions and depend on others to point the way.

When you release Cancer and Capricorn's shadow sides, you can become completely present with yourself. You can feel your connection with everyone around you and the wisdom of the Universe. You become clear in your energy and know the direction to take next. You are in touch with your priorities and make sure your self-care is one of them. You achieve a true work/life balance that isn't black or white. You understand the importance your life's work and know that it will infiltrate everything you do. You also understand, though, how to take a break energetically from your work. You can set boundaries with yourself, knowing that when you replenish your spirit, everything else in your life benefits.

The balance of Capricorn and Cancer also allows you to lead others with integrity. You know who you are and show up as that person in every situation with reverence for yourself. You also know how to make decisions based on what is most important to your soul's mission. Most importantly, you know how to find your way home if you become lost. On this Full Moon, bring awareness to what you need to shift to achieve the balance of Capricorn's and Cancer's energies in your life.

The following practices are designed to help you integrate the higher vibrations of Capricorn and Cancer. Take your time with them and allow the answers to arrive naturally.

CAPRICORN PRACTICES

1. How is your work/life balance? Are you spending too much time on one aspect of your life and not enough on others?

CAPRICORN PRACTICES

2. What helps you understand your core essence? What helps you understand what is most important to you?

_____

_____

_____

_____

_____

_____

_____

_____

_____

_____

_____

_____

_____

_____

_____

_____

_____

_____

_____

_____

_____

_____

_____

_____

_____

_____

CAPRICORN PRACTICES

3. Have you found your life's work? If yes, does it still inspire you? If no, what do you need to release to make space for it to appear?

CAPRICORN PRACTICES

4. What does internal work look like for you? What are you trying to break through, and what are you trying to shift?

_____

_____

_____

_____

_____

_____

_____

_____

_____

_____

_____

_____

_____

_____

_____

_____

_____

_____

_____

_____

_____

_____

_____

_____

_____

_____

_____

_____

CAPRICORN PRACTICES

5. What distracts you from your work? What brings your attention back to your priorities when you have lost your focus?

CAPRICORN PRACTICES

6. How do you define self-care? How do you define productivity? Where can these two paths connect?

_____

_____

_____

_____

_____

_____

_____

_____

_____

_____

_____

_____

_____

_____

_____

_____

_____

_____

_____

_____

_____

_____

_____

_____

_____

_____

_____

_____

_____

CAPRICORN PRACTICES

7. When you make time for yourself, how do you benefit? How do others around you benefit?

_____

_____

_____

_____

_____

_____

_____

_____

_____

_____

_____

_____

_____

_____

_____

_____

_____

_____

_____

_____

_____

_____

_____

_____

CAPRICORN PRACTICES

8. Where in your life are you showing up as yourself? Where, or how, are you hiding your truth?

_____

_____

_____

_____

_____

_____

_____

_____

_____

_____

_____

_____

_____

_____

_____

_____

_____

_____

_____

_____

_____

_____

_____

_____

_____

_____

_____

CAPRICORN PRACTICES

9. What do you need to release to live in your truth? Fear? Shame? Something else?

_____

_____

_____

_____

_____

_____

_____

_____

_____

_____

_____

_____

_____

_____

_____

_____

_____

_____

_____

_____

_____

_____

_____

CAPRICORN PRACTICES

10. What practices can you commit to this Full Moon that will help you find your truth and align with your life's work?

_____

_____

_____

_____

_____

_____

_____

_____

_____

_____

_____

_____

_____

_____

_____

_____

_____

_____

_____

_____

_____

_____

_____

_____

LAST QUARTER: IN ARIES

JULY 1

Last Quarter Moons occur when the Moon squares the Sun or is exactly 90 degrees away from it. This angle is what creates our Half Moon. Square aspects feel like friction in our lives. The Last Quarter square illuminates energy that is holding us back, bringing it to the forefront of our consciousness. The tension we feel is often within the interacting energies of the Moon and Sun signs. The opportunity of every square is to break through the pressure and create a higher vibration between the energies involved.

This Last Quarter Moon is in Aries, while the Sun remains in Cancer. Aries brings energy to the emotional body, stirring up feelings. It can make us feel restless, impatient, and even frustrated with ourselves and others. Be aware if any of these emotions are coming up for you, and direct your internal fire toward something productive instead of destructive.

Harness the fire provided by Aries to become clear about what aligns with your authentic self and what is merely a mask adjusted for society. Get in touch with what makes you feel alive, what makes you jump out of bed in the morning, and what truly motivates you. Alignment with the soul is the power of Aries. This energy shows us our inner fire and teaches us how to keep it burning.

Aries's energy needs motion. So move your body throughout the day.. Do something that makes you remember how much you love life. Feel your passions and what sets your soul of fire. Then direct that fire to burn up anything you don't want in your energy, your mind, and your life. Make a list of the energies you are not taking into the next cycle and burn it (safely). Watch the words melt off the paper onto the Earth to be made anew, clearing space within your energetic field for new vibrations. Continue to release what doesn't completely resonate with your soul's journey until the next New Moon in Cancer.

What are you willing to let go this Last Quarter Moon to allow yourself to receive new energy?

AFFIRMATIONS

Think of people in your life, or in the world, who live an authentic life, full of integrity. What qualities do these people possess? Write down as many that come to mind when you envision this type of person.

Now write yourself three - five affirmations using the qualities you listed above. Create "I am statements" which you can tell yourself when the world pulls you from your center.